Creative Start Books

There's a Mouse in the House!

Written by: Elisabeth Lanelle

Co-Written & Illustrated by:

____

(Your Name)

Today, when I got home from school, I washed my hands and went into the kitchen to get a snack. I picked ___________________.

It is one of my favorite snacks!

This is what it looked like:

After I finished my snack, I started to play

_________________________________ because

_________________________________.

All of a sudden, SLAM! I heard the kitchen cupboard door close. It was so loud!

This was the look on my face when I heard it:

I went into the kitchen to see what made that loud noise! It was A MOUSE!

It looked like this:

The mouse looked hungry. So, I gave the

mouse some cheese. Then, I named the

mouse:

______________________________.

My friend _______________, the mouse,

felt much better after the cheese. So, it ran

out into the backyard where they lived with

their family of mice in the flower garden.

Look at all the pretty flowers in the garden:

Now, every time I go outside into the backyard, I wave hello to my mouse friends who live in the garden.

See me waving "Hello" :

I think the next book we write should be

about

____

____

And the Cover of the book should look like

this:

Elisabeth Lanelle

2022

There's a Mouse in the House! is a part of the *Creative Start Books* Series. Where kids get to help write and fully illustrate so they choose how they want their book to look!

Hey Friends! Did you like getting to help write and illustrate your own book? Elisabeth likes to write and color books too! If you have any ideas for the next topic she should write about – have your parent or guardian send her a message on Etsy or post on Instagram with the hashtag #creativestartbooks with your idea and you might get to see a book made just for you!

Elisabeth is a Nurse! She also loves to write books in her free time. She has created diaries and journals, along with the Creative Start Books Series, for Kids, Teens, and Adults with blank lines – Just to write down whatever they would like to write.

Elisabeth wants to remind you to make sure to keep your creative ideas flowing. It can be one of the most fun ways to express yourself!

On these next 8 pages, you can choose to write or color whatever you would like! Maybe you can even write your own short story!

The End!